H**Help!**W DO I KNOW GOD'S WILL?

A JESUS-CENTERED GUIDE

A JESUS-CENTERED GUIDE

HELP! HOW DO I KNOW GOD'S WILL?

Copyright © 2018 Group Publishing, Inc./0000 0001 0362 4853

Lifetree™ is an imprint of Group Publishing, Inc.

Visit our website: group.com

Written by Mikal Keefer

Library of Congress Cataloging-in-Publication Data

Names: Group Publishing.
Title: Help! How do I know God's will?
Description: First American paperback [edition]. | Loveland, Colorado : Group
   Publishing, Inc., 2018. | Series: A Jesus-centered guide
Identifiers: LCCN 2017052346 (print) | LCCN 2017055284 (ebook) | ISBN
   9781470753252 (ePub) | ISBN 9781470753245 (pbk.)
Subjects: LCSH: God (Christianity)--Will. | Discernment (Christian theology)
   | Listening--Religious aspects--Christianity. | Spiritual
   journals--Authorship. | Diaries--Authorship--Religious
   aspects--Christianity.
Classification: LCC BT135 (ebook) | LCC BT135 .H355 2018 (print) | DDC
   248.4--dc23
LC record available at https://lccn.loc.gov/2017052346

ISBN: 978-1-4707-5324-5 (softcover)

ISBN: 978-1-4707-5325-2 (ePub)

Printed in the United States of America.

10 9 8 7 6 5 4 3 2 1   27 26 25 24 23 22 21 20 19 18

TABLE OF CONTENTS

INTRODUCTION

If God wants you to do his will, why is it so hard to know exactly what he's after?

He's great with the big picture stuff—don't murder or cheat, be nice to people—but annoyingly thin on details.

Who should you marry? What about that job in Boston—take it or leave it? And is buying a house in this market a great idea or the worst financial decision ever?

You want to do God's will. Really. If *he'd just answer your questions.*

Because that's the rub, right? You bump up against a decision and ask God what he wants you to do. Then you ask again…and again.

And you hear nothing. Not a peep.

So hear this: God *does* care. He *is* listening. You *can* know his will and—if you choose—do it.

And this little pocket guide will help.

Not that you're holding a formula for uncovering God's Word. Rather, these are lessons learned by people who have tackled the same question you're asking: *How do I know and follow God's will?*

They're sharing what's helped them, and it's good advice. But it's only advice—not a recipe for you to follow.

How God makes his will known to you may be vastly different from how he makes his will known to someone else. But that's okay. That's part of the fun, a slice of the adventure.

So relax. Take a deep breath.

You don't need a seminary degree or silent month in a monastery to discern God's will. You already have exactly what you need: a willing heart, a deep desire, and a God who wants nothing more than to connect with you in life-changing ways.

Pretty much all you're missing, if you want to get the most from this book, is a pen—you'll do a bit of journaling—and a few minutes to read, write, and pray.

The journaling is so you can see how your story unfolds. That's helpful. Equally helpful is a Bible that's easy to understand and keeps your attention focused on Jesus—because knowing him is at the very heart of knowing God's will. More about that later.

So, if you're ready, so are we.

Let's dive in.

"
True friendship
can afford true
knowledge.
It does not depend
on darkness and
ignorance.
"

—*Henry David Thoreau*

IT'S ALL ABOUT RELATIONSHIP

Cindy's an IRS agent so, come tax time, she hears from *lots* of people.

"Calls usually start with, 'How are you? How are Rick and the kids? We should get together sometime. Hey, since I have you on the line, is there any way pet food is deductible?'"

Cindy's learned that nobody's really interested in hearing about her family. Once she answers whatever question prompted the call, there's an awkward silence, a "gotta run," and the line goes dead. And getting together? It never happens.

"Some years I'd give anything to just get a call asking me to go out for coffee," Cindy says. "No hidden agenda. No request for free tax info. Just coffee with a friend."

Cindy's not alone.

God also gets far more calls looking for advice than friendship.

Which is a shame, because God cares *way* more about your friendship than your to-do list. He already knows you're not perfect—that's why God sent Jesus. That's why there's grace and forgiveness.

Besides, he's already crazy about you. You don't have to earn his love.

So rather than worry about always doing The Right Thing, focus on having an ever-deepening friendship with God. As you draw closer to him, you'll get to know him better, and that will help you know his will.

Because that's how it works with friends. Sooner or later you know not just who they are, but what they value. And, if you love them, you're eager to please them.

Augustine, a theologian in the early church, summed it up this way: "Love God and do what you will."

He was on to something.

Rather than think of God as a boss barking orders at you—"Marry Dan, become an accountant, buy the Volvo"—Augustine urges you to love God and then work it out from there...together.

Sort of like a married couple who operate from a base of mutual trust and respect. They make decisions together, honoring each other in the process. They begin by loving each other and wanting to please each other.

And then they decide: Will the kitchen be painted Twilight Blue or Azure Cream Blue? Or maybe French Cloudless Summer Sky Blue with a hint of Tuscan Lake tossed in?

There's great stress in always fretting about doing The Right Thing, and refreshing, delightful joy in simply diving deeply into a friendship with God. Of course, in this particular friendship, God's intentions and perspective and imperatives carry tremendous weight—he's not shy about raising issues of "obedience" with us. But it's an obedience born out of intimacy and respect, not rote religious rule-keeping.

So, by all means, ask God what you should do. He's not trying to withhold information from you and welcomes a conversation with you about anything you choose to bring up.

Just make sure you stop by for coffee now and then, too.

Because that's what friends do.

PEN-IN-HAND PONDERING

In what ways is your relationship with God like a friendship to you, and in what ways is it more like a servant/master relationship?

Think about the last few times you've prayed or reached out to God. Of course, we are often asking him for help, but what are some hurdles you face when you think of interacting with him more broadly as a friend?

_____

_____

_____

_____

_____

_____

_____

_____

_____

What are some important characteristics about your close friends that prompt you to trust them and be vulnerable with them? In what ways do you see these characteristics in God, and in what ways do you not see those characteristics?

What are the similarities and differences between your relationship with God and your closest human relationship? Explain.

_____

_____

_____

_____

_____

_____

_____

_____

_____

_____

_____

TALK WITH GOD ABOUT IT

Do you even *want* to draw closer to God? Some people don't—they're happy to keep God right where they've got him.

Tell God why you are...or aren't...interested in deepening your friendship. And listen to what he has to say about it.

DO THIS Ask God to help you find something small in nature that reminds you of your friendship with him. A vibrant, healthy leaf, perhaps. Or a broken twig. Or a small, flat rock. Whatever it is, press it between these pages and let it be a reminder of where you are today.

GET TO KNOW JESUS

Jenn is a *huge* Alice Cooper fan.

She grew up listening to Cooper's music—that raspy voice snarling about teenage angst, a heavy-metal wall of sound that perfectly reflected Jenn's darkest moments.

"And his stage show is spectacular," Jenn says. "Guillotines, snakes, decapitated baby dolls—there's fake blood spurting everywhere. And striding through the middle of it comes Alice, black makeup framing the wildest eyes I've ever seen."

Jenn spent years devouring every word Alice wrote and every interview that appeared in print.

And then she met Alice. Not in a crowded green room after a concert, but at an event where she actually talked with him.

"He was wearing plaid golf pants, a polo shirt, and a perky little golf cap," says Jenn. "Not a trace of makeup. He looked like my uncle Larry."

Plus, there was none of the raging maniac. "He was just this nice, normal guy. And I realized that, while I knew all *about* Alice, I certainly didn't *know* Alice."

Jenn tumbled onto a truth that can help you know God's will: It's one thing to study God and another to spend time with him. They're not remotely the same.

And there's no better way to spend time with God than by spending time with Jesus.

Jesus said this to his followers: "I am the way, the truth, and the life. No one can come to the Father except through me. If you had really known me, you would know who my Father is. From now on, you do know him and have seen him!" (John 14:6-7).

If you're trying to sort out God's will for your life without involving Jesus, you've missed a huge opportunity. God has made a way for us to understand his heart, and that way's name is "The Way," or Jesus.

Pay attention to Jesus as he's described in the Bible. Watch how he makes decisions. See what he considers important, how he yields to God's guidance.

Jesus models perfectly what it is to navigate a life in tune with God's will.

And he's willing to help you do the same.

Why wouldn't you take him up on his offer?

PEN-IN-HAND PONDERING

Would you say you're more of a student of Jesus or a friend of Jesus? Why do you answer as you do?

What's one word that best describes Jesus to you? Why do you choose that word, and how does that word help or hinder your ability to know him more intimately?

Jesus asked his disciples to tell him what people were saying about him—how do you think most people in our culture feel about Jesus, and why? How is your perspective about Jesus different from the assumptions about him in the culture?

TALK WITH GOD ABOUT IT

Here's what *doesn't* help you know Jesus better: shame that you haven't done more to understand him in the past. That just muddies the waters and clouds your way forward.

Talk with God about this: What can the two of you do together in the next few days that will help you see him more clearly? And what does God want to show you about himself through the person of Jesus?

DO THIS Read this passage aloud at least twice: "I am the way, the truth, and the life. No one can come to the Father except through me. If you had really known me, you would know who my Father is. From now on, you do know him and have seen him!" (John 14:6-7).

What, if anything, in Jesus' words makes you uncomfortable or confused? In what ways do they comfort you?

There's no substitute for connecting with Jesus if you want to know God's will for your life. A friendship with Jesus *is* God's will for your life...but you've got to take him as he is, not as you'd like him to be, or as others insist he is.

If you're uncertain where you stand with Jesus, pick up your phone and call someone who seems to know Jesus pretty well—someone who knows you and really loves Jesus. Someone willing to talk with you about your view of Jesus.

Ask Jesus who to call, and then do it.

And if you can't think of a spiritual mentor to call, call your mother. She hasn't heard from you in a while.

"

There's both
an art and a science
to asking questions.
The science is asking
the right question
of the right person.
The art is listening
deeply to the
answer.

"

—*Gabriel Mason*

ASK THE RIGHT QUESTION

Sheila counsels women who want to lose weight. And she never begins a counseling relationship by asking how many pounds someone wants to shed.

"That's the wrong question," says Sheila. "It's better to ask, 'What sort of life do you want to live after losing weight?' Maybe it's keeping up with her kids at the playground. Or finally taking that hiking vacation in Ireland."

Sheila knows that if you want to temporarily fit into a dress for the class reunion, you focus on pounds. But if you're looking for a transformed life, you focus on what that life will be like.

"Asking the right question changes everything," says Sheila.

When we want to know God's will, we often ask, "What do you want me to do?"

But the better question is, "Who are you making me into?"

That second question gives God room to shape you and keeps the long game in mind. You may not hear an answer to a specific question—whether to end a relationship, for instance. But the experience of asking God to shape you through a time of uncertainty is powerful, and helps shift your focus from short-term relief to long-term freedom in your life.

You hear best from God in the context of a friendship, an ongoing conversation that ebbs and flows. You develop an intimacy that makes room for you to view God as more than Tech Support—that number you call only when things go wrong.

Sheila's question lifts her clients' sights from a problem to be solved to a life to be lived. It provides vision and fuels hope.

Asking the right question of God does the same for you.

He's shaping you for eternity, not just to pass through an immediate crisis.

When your car's transmission locks up and you can't afford to fix it, of course you cry out to God, asking what to do. That's just human.

Just be aware that the best part isn't his giving you an answer. The best part is that he's intending to use these circumstances to bring greater joy and trust in your life, because the two of you are walking through car-related aggravation together.

PEN-IN-HAND PONDERING

Write about a time you asked Jesus what to do about something and got an answer. What prompted your question—and what did you do with the answer?

If you could ask Jesus any question and be sure of getting a crystal-clear response, what would you ask? Why that question?

_____

_____

_____

_____

_____

_____

_____

_____

_____

_____

TALK WITH GOD ABOUT IT

Grab a pencil and blank sheet of paper; then find a quiet spot.

Ask God what, if anything, he's wanted to tell you that you've been too distracted to hear. Maybe you've even been so tightly focused on one concern that you've missed the larger picture of what he's trying to teach you.

Doodle…jot words that float into your mind…draw an image that comes to mind. Be open to listening, not just through your ears but also through your fingers.

Ask Jesus what question he wishes you would ask him; then ask him.

DO THIS Questions are powerful.

Today, in your conversations, make a point of asking more follow-up questions than you usually do. When a friend or co-worker shares a story, dig a little deeper. See what a difference asking the right question can make in your relationships.

With friends. With family. With work buddies. With God.

EXPECT A RESPONSE

When Jayden wrote to the president of the United States, the last thing he expected was what he got: an actual response.

"And not one of those auto-pen pictures," Jayden says. "It was a letter dictated and then hand-signed by the president."

Jayden had invited the president to a testimonial dinner Jayden was hosting for a community leader. Jayden expected a form letter offering regrets that he could give to the honoree as a joke.

"When the president writes to you, it's a big deal," says Jayden. Because the letter became part of a presidential archive, he had to provide details about the person being honored, the event, even about himself.

"I didn't have all the information the White House needed when they called," says Jayden. "I hadn't expected a response, so I wasn't prepared when I got one."

Jayden presented the president's letter to the guest of honor at the event. "It was the highlight of the evening," says Jayden. "It may have been the highlight of her *life*."

Call it anticipation. *Divine* anticipation.

When you ask God for wisdom and guidance, are you expecting a response? If not, why be surprised if a response slips past you when it comes?

If you're not hearing Jesus speak when you ask him about his will for your life, here are two practical truths to keep in mind:

1. He's probably not shouting.

2. He may have already told you what he thinks.

About volume: Jesus tends not to turn it up very loud. He's often subtle when making suggestions, preferring the two of you talk them over rather than issuing an edict you can't ignore. It's all about the relationship, remember?

And perhaps he's already been clear about his stand on what you're suggesting. Thinking about fudging the numbers on your tax return? That's pretty well covered in the Ten Commandments.

James wrote this: "If you need wisdom, ask our generous God, and he will give it to you…But when you ask him, be sure that your faith is in God alone. Do not waver, for a person with divided loyalty is as unsettled as a wave of the sea that is blown and tossed by the wind" (James 1:5-6).

In other words, expect a response from God.

Just not necessarily the way you expect to get it…or the response you are hoping for.

And practical tip 3: It's probably going to involve the two of you having a discussion.

PEN-IN-HAND PONDERING

On a scale from 1 to 10, with 1 representing "not much" and 10 representing "very much," how much do you expect Jesus to actually give you guidance when you ask for wisdom and insight? What's shaped your level of expectation?

What's one trusted way of knowing you've received help or guidance from Jesus?

What's one way God seems to speak to you most often? Why do you think he chooses that particular way with you?

TALK WITH GOD ABOUT IT

First, know that if you're not happy with God for some reason, it's okay to tell him. He can take it. So it's okay to be honest.

Tell Jesus how you're feeling about his record of responding when you pray. If you're delighted, say so. If you're disappointed, explain why.

Open up the conversation. You may be surprised by what you hear in response.

DO THIS Tell Jesus about something that's important in your life right now. Ask him for the wisdom he can provide. But do this: pray in a whisper, as often as you think about it. Keep whispering. He'll hear you.

Then, throughout the next day or two, keep an eye open for his response through a nudge in one direction or another. An insight shared by a friend. A thought or image popping into your mind.

Expect a response—it *will* be coming.

"

People cheer
the Bible, buy the Bible,
give the Bible,
own the Bible—
they just don't actually
read the Bible.

"

—*John Ortberg*

KNOW WHAT
GOD'S ALREADY SAID

Maybe it's because Chris is a guy, but the last thing he reads when he's assembling anything is the instruction sheet.

"I glance at the diagram, and that's enough," he says, though an entertainment center he once put together might disagree.

Chris laid out the pre-cut parts of the unit, grabbed his toolbox, and got busy. "This thing was *huge*," Chris remembers. "It took forever getting it together."

Not helpful were the occasional remarks from his wife that it didn't look quite right. Chris pressed on, and it wasn't until he pushed the unit against the wall that he realized the shelving was installed backward. Every finished shelf edge was facing the wall, and all that was visible from the living room was particle board.

"I was seriously considering just painting the edging," says Chris. "But my wife had seen it all. She'd warned me something was wrong, but I hadn't listened.

"I had no choice but to take it all apart and start over…as she watched."

Not Chris' finest moment…but quite the learning experience.

If you want to know how to do something, don't reinvent the wheel. Take a look at what's already been figured out and benefit from it.

For instance: You're not the first person to ask what God's will for your life is.

And by far the most qualified person to answer that question is none other than Jesus, who said: "'You must love the Lord your God with all your heart, all your soul, and all your mind.' This is the first and greatest commandment. A second is equally important: 'Love your neighbor as yourself'" (Matthew 22:37-39).

Honoring those two values puts guardrails around pretty much any decision you could make.

Thinking about joining the weekend soccer league? Will it generally help or hinder loving God "with all your heart, soul, and mind"? In what way will it help you love the people in your life?

And if you'd like to dig deeper, get to know the Bible. It's *packed* with examples of decisions and their consequences.

Plus, experienced Jesus-followers can't recommend the Bible highly enough.

Here's what Paul told his young friend, Timothy: "All Scripture is inspired by God and is useful to teach us what is true and to make us realize what is wrong in our lives. It corrects us when we are wrong and teaches us to do what is right. God uses it to prepare and equip his people to do every good work" (2 Timothy 3:16-17).

You may not find a step-by-step diagram showing you God's will for your life in the Bible, but you'll get a sense of how to grow in your friendship with God... and what kind of decisions build that friendship. And you'll see the heart behind Jesus' influence and guidance in others' lives—when you understand his heart better, you'll understand his will better.

PEN-IN-HAND PONDERING

What three words would you use to describe how you feel about the Bible? Looking at what you wrote, what sort of picture do those words paint?

Think about something right now in your life that you need God's guidance in—what's something you already know about God's will that can shed light on your situation? Explain.

TALK WITH GOD ABOUT IT

Some people think the best way to get to know Jesus is through mastering the Bible. But think about every other significant relationship in your life: Has it grown best by studying the other person or by spending time with that person? Unless we're talking mail-order brides, it's spending time.

So ask Jesus for new and creative and doable ways the two of you could spend more time together without it involving closing your eyes and bowing your head. What other options are available? Talk it over, listen, and notice what pops into your head.

DO THIS Whatever you and God just decided about time together? Go do that…but also consider spending time in the Bible. Not all of it—just the parts that are most relevant to your life right now. The rest you can read later.

For example, read Paul's letter to the Philippians for practical help on living in community with other broken people like yourself. Or take a quick glance through the book of Mark, stopping often to see how Jesus interacted with needy people; that will tell you a lot. Then read the book of John and focus on what

Jesus said to different groups of people—ask yourself why he talks the way he does with diverse people.

Pause often to invite Jesus to speak into your life. Say, "Show me how this can help me know you better, Jesus. And, through you, God's will for my life."

You'll probably hear plenty, so take notes in the margins of your Bible.

> **"**
> The Lord does whatever pleases him throughout all heaven and earth, and on the seas and in their depths.
> **"**
>
> *Psalm 135:6*

BE OKAY
WITH EXCLAMATION POINTS

Michael still hasn't recovered...not completely.
"I was raised thinking you figured out God's will by reading the Bible," he says. "God didn't actually *talk* to you. Anything that didn't come with a Scripture reference was highly suspect."

So imagine Michael's surprise when, while seated at a concert, he "heard" a voice say, "Go talk to that man."

Michael says it was an audible voice, but nobody around him heard it. And as his head swiveled to the right, he knew exactly who the voice had in mind: a dejected-looking guy sitting off to the side of the concert venue.

"I got up and made my way toward him—much to the dismay of others in the audience whose view I blocked en route. And when I got there, a woman also walked up. She'd also heard a voice…but she was far less distressed about it."

Michael believes God spoke to him—and in a way that rattled his theology and opened up new avenues for Michael to hear God speak.

"God was rallying the troops to help the guy we prayed with," says Michael. "But in the process, he took care of me, too. I discovered God can speak through exclamation points, not just footnotes."

Is it such a stretch to imagine that God still speaks to his friends?

It was for Michael, but since then he's discovered that Jesus makes his will known in all sorts of ways. In dreams, in prophetic words spoken by others, in moments when a thought occurs for no apparent reason.

These can all be ways Jesus makes his will known. To spark a conversation with us.

But it's *also* true that those images and words might spring from our own subconscious or from darker spiritual places.

How can you know the difference?

Here's a quick litmus test: How do you feel about the message you're receiving? If it's empowering, Jesus-honoring, and consistent with his character and mission, it's worth considering and checking against what you know of God's will as he's expressed it in Scripture and in the person of Jesus.

Paul, who had his share of direct encounters with God, wrote this to his young friend, Timothy: "For God has not given us a spirit of fear and timidity, but of power, love, and self-discipline" (2 Timothy 1:7).

If that's what you're feeling as you consider your exclamation-point encounter, don't brush it off. Ponder it. Consider giving it permission to shape your actions.

Perhaps Jesus is reaching out to you.

PEN-IN-HAND PONDERING

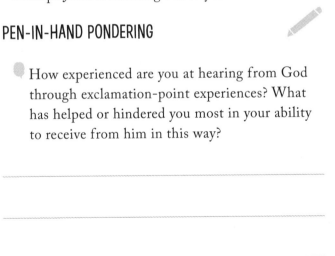

How experienced are you at hearing from God through exclamation-point experiences? What has helped or hindered you most in your ability to receive from him in this way?

If you've ever heard directly from Jesus about something he wants you to do, describe that experience here. If you've never had that experience, what are the possible reasons that hasn't happened?

TALK WITH GOD ABOUT IT

Perhaps you know someone who steadfastly refuses to send or receive text messages. Or tweets. Or even hand-written letters. They've cut off communication through those venues and—no surprise—nobody tries to connect with them in those ways.

Ask Jesus if you've cut off some avenue through which he might like to connect with you. If so, what is it—and how willing are you to open up that channel of communication?

DO THIS Before you go to bed tonight, put a paper, pen, and a light source within easy reach. If you awake and can recall a dream, jot it down quickly—before it fades. Then, later, review it and ask if God was reaching out to you through your dream.

The answer may be no, and that's fine.

But what if the answer is yes?

REMOVE OBSTACLES

It started so gradually that Bob hardly noticed.

First it was a vague reverb that sometimes happened when certain people spoke to him. Nothing big, but there it was…and it was troubling.

Especially troubling when Bob found himself leaning into conversations, focusing to catch words, and watching lips as people spoke.

And then came the vertigo.

Aware his hearing was fading, knowing deafness was closing in on him like an unwelcome shroud, Bob scheduled an appointment with the best ear, nose, and throat doctor he could find.

After Bob described his symptoms, the doctor examined Bob's ears.

Bob knew what the doctor must be seeing: scarred eardrums. A raging infection. Perhaps delicate, broken bones protruding from his inner ear.

But the doctor calmly reached into a cabinet, pulled out a squirt bottle with a thin hose attached, and quickly irrigated Bob's ears.

"Enough earwax poured out to make a life-size mold of my head," says Bob, who quickly realized his only problem was excessive earwax.

His hearing was fine. "Once the obstacles were removed, I could hear everything—including the price for the five minutes the doctor spent helping me. *That* I heard loud and clear."

If you're not hearing from God, it doesn't necessarily mean he's gone silent. He may be speaking, but something's keeping you from hearing him.

Occasionally God wraps messages in thunderbolts to get your attention, and those are hard to miss. But he usually communicates in far less dramatic ways.

Good advice from a friend. A Bible verse that seems to leap off the page. A clear set of circumstances. A Scripture reference that pops into your head, and you go there to discover just the right word you need right now.

God can be—and often is—in all of those.

And then there's his favorite: A thought comes to mind as the two of you have a conversation, or a gentle word gives you his take on a situation you face.

Those are easy to miss if you've let something get in the way of hearing him clearly.

Maybe you've chosen to distance yourself so you can chase after something other than God. Or you won't let go of unhealthy beliefs and attitudes or set aside plans you've hatched that pull you away from God.

God's in this with you, remember? Having the freedom to come to him means you also have the freedom to turn away. It's up to you. God's not likely to smash through walls you've raised between the two of you or push through your apathy or anger.

He'll simply love you. Invite you to wade deeper into the cool, refreshing waters of your friendship to become who he's created you to be.

If you're not hearing God, it's worth asking: Are there obstacles between the two of you that he wants to remove?

PEN-IN-HAND PONDERING

Thinking about your relationships with people, what gets in the way of clearly hearing what they say? List those obstacles here:

Now, looking at what you wrote, how are those obstacles like or unlike what you experience with God?

_____

_____

_____

_____

_____

_____

_____

_____

_____

What's something you could change about your life that would likely deepen your friendship with Jesus but you're reluctant to do? Ask yourself an honest question: Why?

TALK WITH GOD ABOUT IT

Sometimes when a human friendship cools, it stays that way because everyone involved is too embarrassed to reconnect. Easier to pretend that the new normal is okay, that the distance is fine all around.

If that's happened with you and Jesus, it's not because he stopped caring. But he does respect you. If you want to turn into a Christmas card/Facebook birthday thumbs-up friend, he'll let you do that. But like any close friend who senses distance in the relationship, that's going to grieve him. That's not the intimacy he's after—not with you. Not with someone he loves as much as he loves you.

If you sense distance, risk connecting. Ask him what he's been up to in your life.

The two of you can take it from there.

 Grab a washcloth and see what sort of earwax has been accumulating in your ears while you were busy focusing on other things. Doctors generally agree it's a bad idea to shove cotton swabs down in your ear canal, so don't go that route.

You're still likely to discover there's ample earwax between you and hearing clearly.

As you perform this DIY procedure, consider what might be preventing you from hearing God right now in your life. Ask Jesus to show you what it is and give you the determination to do something about it.

CONSIDER YOUR CIRCUMSTANCES

Olivia and Aiden had zero doubt about their future. They knew they'd been called to the mission field, so shortly after they married each other, they moved in with friends, gave up their jobs, and dove into fundraising.

"We gave ourselves six months to raise the support we needed," says Aiden. If they made it—as they were sure they would—they'd take it as a sign they should head overseas.

If they fell short, they'd find jobs and jump back into work stateside.

After six months they hadn't quite raised all the money. "We were close but not there," says Olivia. Taking the missed deadline as a test of their faith, they pledged to give the effort another 30 days. Then back to work.

Thirty days later they still hadn't met budget. They faced a decision: Was coming in short of their goal God's way of telling them to stay put? Or was Satan throwing an obstacle in their way? Or was it something else?

Their entire future rested on deciphering their circumstances...and they didn't have a clue.

Olivia and Aiden aren't alone. Determining God's will based on our circumstances is tough—and often far from precise.

That's why it's almost never a good idea to rely on circumstances alone when seeking guidance. Our would-be missionary friends are right: Challenging times may be a signal it's time to choose another path. Other times those same challenges are confirmation that we're right where we need to be.

So how do you tell the difference?

Do this: Ask mature believers to help you interpret your situation. See if one resolution or another leads you to feel peace rather than conflict. Jesus told a story to teach his disciples about prayer—it's a story about a guy who knocks on a friend's door at midnight, asking for a few loaves of bread to feed unexpected guests. The friend is in bed, doesn't want to get up. But because the guy keeps knocking, his friend finally gets up and gives him what he needs. So keep knocking on his door until he gives you clarity.

Pay attention to Jesus—*ridiculous* attention to Jesus. Listen carefully. How is he speaking to you in the midst of your circumstances? Give it some time, and you'll see your path open up before you.

Though it's never a good idea to rely solely on circumstances for guidance, neither is it wise to ignore them. It's the tuition you pay as you learn from your master rabbi, Jesus. It just makes sense to benefit as fully as possible from the experience.

PEN-IN-HAND PONDERING

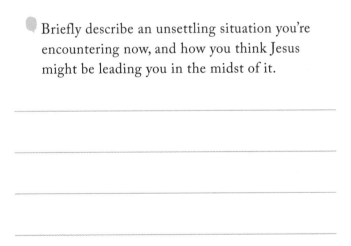

Briefly describe an unsettling situation you're encountering now, and how you think Jesus might be leading you in the midst of it.

If you decided to "pay ridiculous attention to Jesus," what's one thing you'd have to do differently? Where do you tend to see Jesus at work in the world and in your life?

If Olivia and Aiden were to call and ask for your take on their situation, what would you tell them? What experiences or insights drive your advice?

TALK WITH GOD ABOUT IT

When circumstances are uncomfortable, we tend not to spend time mulling them over, sifting them for lessons we might learn.

We want them to change...*now.*

Have a conversation with Jesus about the unsettling situation you described. Ask if there's something buried in your situation that is guiding you back to him. Ask him to help you learn what he's trying to teach.

 Grab a handful of pennies to carry with you the next day or two, or until you run through your pile of pennies.

When you find yourself in a situation that might give you an opportunity to grow closer to God, place a penny wherever it happens. Missed an elevator and now you're stuck waiting for two minutes, two minutes you could use to pray for others who are waiting? That's penny-worthy...place one on the floor.

At a meeting where you're able to give a reassuring word to a colleague? Leave a penny on the table.

You're training yourself to think about how Jesus might be speaking to you through circumstances, and it's just a penny per lesson. What a deal!

> "
> Create in me
> a clean heart, O God.
> Renew a loyal spirit
> within me.
> "
>
> *Psalm 51:10*

RENEW YOUR MIND

Susan was feeling pretty cocky about her ability to communicate when her plane touched down in Mexico City. She had three years of high school Spanish under her belt and a semester of classes lined up at a Mexican university, and she was ready to rock.

Her confidence lasted about five minutes.

"There's a world of difference between classroom Spanish and what cabbies speak," she says. "I couldn't keep up, and the constant translating made my head feel like it was going to explode."

Several weeks later, Susan experienced a breakthrough.

A classmate told a joke, and Susan burst out laughing, effortlessly joining in the banter. And it hit her: "I was actually *thinking in Spanish*," she says. "No translating needed—it was like my brain had been rewired!"

When it comes to hearing from God—concerning his will or anything else—a certain amount of rewiring is essential.

We've got to get ready to receive what he wants to tell us.

Paul wrote this: "Don't copy the behavior and customs of this world, but let God transform you into a new person by changing the way you think. Then you will learn to know God's will for you, which is good and pleasing and perfect" (Romans 12:2).

Notice that God's emphasis is on transforming how you *think*, not how you *act*. If your actions change, it won't be because he bullied you into straightening up. That's not how God works.

But he *is* eager to cooperate with you to shift your thinking, helping you draw closer to him and deepening your friendship. That's when real, lasting transformation happens, from the inside out.

If you're wondering how to know and follow God's will, pay careful attention to Paul's words. It's when you experience transformed thinking that you'll know God's will...because you're ready to hear it.

PEN-IN-HAND PONDERING

 You care about knowing God and doing what he wants you to do, so some of the transformation Paul describes has already happened in you. What's one way your thinking changed since you came to know Jesus?

"Good and pleasing and perfect" is how Paul describes God's will for you. Hmm…what three words would *you* choose to describe God's will for you, as you understand it? Why do you choose those words?

Describe a situation to which you'd react differently now than you did 10 years ago. What do you think explains the change?

TALK WITH GOD ABOUT IT

Some say our thoughts, not our emotions, are the essence of who we really are. And God wants to have influence in shaping those thoughts.

Which is sort of what it means to be brainwashed, right?

How willing are you to give God that kind of influence in your life? Do you feel more like an "open book" with him or a "closed book"? Explain.

Have a conversation with Jesus about what's open to him and what—if anything—is off-limits.

 Walk through the place you live and deliberately open every door. As you do, pause at each open door and say aloud, "Renew me, Jesus."

That's the access Jesus wants to have in your life.

What would happen if you gave it to him? Do you trust your friend enough to let him renew you—all of you?

SEEK ADVICE

"The best advice I ever got was to just shut up," says Alex.

Ouch.

Though, to be fair, Alex says he probably deserved it.

He'd left California to attend college in Texas and couldn't stop comparing the two locations—with California always a clear winner. Finally, one of Alex's new college friends looked him in the eyes and said, "If California's so much better, just move your butt back there."

"I took that less as a complaint and more as advice to stop being so critical," says Alex, "to stop focusing on what I didn't like and instead see all the good things that surrounded me."

Taking his friend's advice opened up a new way for Alex to experience his surroundings. And Alex's new attitude of gratitude invited new friendships to grow and blossom.

"It's been a long time since college," says Alex. "But I'm still benefiting from that piece of advice."

Advice is powerful stuff—if you're willing to take it. And if you're humble enough to know you need it.

Jesus wants you to seek his advice when it's time to make decisions. Consider these passages in the Bible: "Fools think their own way is right, but the wise listen to others" (Proverbs 12:15). And there's this: "Plans go wrong for lack of advice; many advisers bring success" (Proverbs 15:22).

It's not that God thinks you're incapable of hearing his voice or making a decision. But he built you for relationship, and one of the huge benefits of relationship is connecting with someone who's been walking with Jesus a bit longer than you. Who's navigated whatever minefield you're in.

That's someone who can give you timely, helpful advice—if you're open to it.

But pick a spiritual mentor wisely. You're looking for someone who's more interested in encouraging you to be a follower of Jesus than a follower of the mentor.

And you're looking for someone who's growing, not someone who thinks he or she has it all figured out.

Because—spoiler alert—we're all on a journey. Nobody's got it all figured out.

PEN-IN-HAND PONDERING

Typically, are you the sort of person who seeks others' advice? Why or why not? What's shaped your attitude toward advice?

Who do you turn to for advice about your life with Jesus, if anyone? Why do you turn to this person?

_____

_____

_____

_____

_____

_____

_____

_____

_____

Describe a time that taking advice was a huge help...or a disaster. What did you learn about advice from the experience?

_____

_____

_____

_____

_____

_____

_____

_____

_____

_____

TALK WITH GOD ABOUT IT

Like it or not, one way Jesus shares his will with you is through other people—that's why the community of his followers is called the body of Christ. So consider now who you can trust to have honest conversations with about tough stuff. Who do you trust as a mature, caring believer who's actively seeking Jesus?

A *great* sign you're talking to the right person is if he or she raises an eyebrow and says: "Hey, I'm not perfect. Shouldn't you be talking to someone else?"

Once you've got someone in mind, talk it over with Jesus. See what he thinks about your choice. Maybe he's got someone else in mind for you.

DO THIS If you and Jesus do come up with a possible mentor, pick up your phone and make the call. Ask if you can buy the person a coffee and ask for some advice.

And when you show up for coffee, be ready to discuss a specific topic. See how the two of you get along. See how comfortable the other person is giving advice, and how much the advice you hear reminds you of what God might say.

This may be the start of a beautiful relationship.

HONOR YOUR DESIRES

Maria grew up loving animals...and feeling guilty.

"I was raised to think serving God was all about full-time ministry," she says. "Pastors, Christian education directors, youth leaders—they're the people who were *really* serving God."

But veterinarians? How could Maria pursue the will of God in her profession? Healing people looked like ministry. Neutering cats? Not so much.

And that's when it hit her: Jesus had given Maria a desire to work with animals, but *people* showed up in her office, too. Stressed people. Worried people. People dealing with the imminent death of a dear friend who just happened to have four legs.

Plus, every time she relieved the suffering of a puppy—that was a good thing, too.

"God put me in this place as surely as he puts some people in pulpits," she says. "His will is done through everyone, not just preachers and teachers."

Sometimes, like Maria, you can get a sense of Jesus' will by paying attention to how he wired you. What are your interests? your skills? What snags your attention every time it comes up in conversation?

What are your desires?

God has an infinite number of possibilities available when crafting his creations, and he paid close attention when he designed you. And, believe it or not, he's delighted with the results.

So be equally open when seeking his will for your life. Trying to pound a square peg into a round hole will not only be frustrating for you; it won't do the peg any favors, either.

The Apostle Paul wrote, "For God is working in you, giving you the desire and the power to do what pleases him" (Philippians 2:13).

Which sounds exactly like finding his will for your life, doesn't it?

So take a tip from Maria: Look for God's will not just *outside* yourself, but *inside* as well. As God gives you a desire to please him, how has he prepared you to do that in a way that's fulfilling?

What are your desires?

PEN-IN-HAND PONDERING

What's a desire you've shelved because it didn't seem practical? What got in the way of pursuing it?

Write down three things that make you unique. If you were telling someone else with those attributes how Jesus might move through those gifts to serve him, what would you say?

Blue-sky it: If you could craft God's will for your life, what would you most like to do?

TALK WITH GOD ABOUT IT

Maria's advice comes with a caution: Some desires lead us in the wrong direction. Eve *really* wanted a bite of that forbidden fruit, and you know how that turned out.

So don't make a decision based on only your desires. Does pursuing a desire lead you to contradict anything Jesus has said is off-limits? That dishonors him or works against his mission in the world? That compromises you or hurts others?

Consider a desire you have right now; get something specific in mind.

Now ask Jesus: How might this desire nudge me toward something you want me to do?

DO THIS Make a list of your desires. You don't have to show it to anyone, so be honest. What has God wired you to do that you'd love, love, love to pursue?

_____

_____

_____

_____

_____

_____

_____

_____

Oops...God was reading over your shoulder after all. So ask him what he thinks about what you wrote.

"

The Lord isn't really
being slow about his promise,
as some people think.
No, he is being patient
for your sake. He does not
want anyone to be destroyed,
but wants everyone
to repent.

"

2 Peter 3:9

CONSULT YOUR
CONSCIENCE

When GPS was young, it wasn't always what you'd call...reliable.

"John was an early user," reports Judy. "He hated reading those fold-up maps we used to carry in our cars. So the idea of plugging in an address, looking at a screen, and seeing exactly where you were and how to get to your destination? He was *all* about that."

Judy didn't trust John's expensive GPS gizmo, especially after one back-road trek they made through the Colorado foothills.

"I was sure we were lost, but John kept pointing to the blinking dot on his GPS screen and saying we were fine. I finally stopped the car so he could look around and see where we were."

John eyed the landscape, consulted the GPS, and after a few long moments, glanced up with a victorious glint in his eye. "See?" he said, pointing to the GPS and a distant road snaking up a mountain. "According to this we're right...over there."

Judy gave him a map for Christmas.

So much for letting GPS be your guide.

And ditto for your conscience.

Both are only as good as the information they've received. Both can deliver pinpoint precision or be wildly off-base. If that happens with your GPS and you get to Grandma's house an hour late, she'll forgive you.

But if your conscience is poorly calibrated, you can wander into serious weeds and not know it until you're in trouble.

God planted an intuition in you that turns you toward him. As you grow in your friendship with God, that intuition—your conscience—becomes both stronger and more finely tuned through the influence of the Holy Spirit.

But if you regularly ignore what your inner GPS is telling you, it fails to function. Paul described some people who habitually disobeyed God this way: "These people are hypocrites and liars, and their consciences are dead" (1 Timothy 4:2).

If you're struggling to discover God's will for your life and know you've been deliberately disobeying him, there's a chance you need to jump-start your conscience. It's not really dead; it's just dormant.

The good news: That jump-start is not only possible, it's doable. You can do it.

Like...right now.

PEN-IN-HAND PONDERING

Maybe you've heard the saying "Let your conscience be your guide." How well has that worked out for you in the past? Why?

Describe a time you felt your conscience kick in and nudge you in one direction or another. What was the situation...and what, if anything, did you do about the nudge?

_____

_____

_____

_____

_____

_____

_____

_____

_____

_____

Describe a time you think your conscience should have kicked in—but didn't. How do you explain that?

TALK WITH GOD ABOUT IT

About that jump-start: It's called repentance.

Big word, but it boils down to this: agreeing with Jesus. Agreeing that whatever you're doing that's seared your conscience is a bad idea. Agreeing with him that turning away from whatever it is will be a better idea.

And agreeing that you'd like Jesus to both forgive you and help you make the change.

Do that and you'll find your conscience is firing up and working fine again.

Ask Jesus if repentance is something he'd like you to experience. Most of us find we need to hit the reset button now and then, to ask Jesus to forgive us as we reaffirm our desire to be close to him.

Perhaps this is your time.

DO THIS Recalibrate your conscience by opening up your personal browser history. Ask God if any of the list of sites you've visited get in the way of your friendship with God or might hurt others. If so, you can expect your conscience to ping.

Getting familiar with that ping—the emotion that comes when your conscience is speaking—is a good thing. You're training yourself to listen to one way you can know God's will.

> **There is nothing more uncommon than common sense.**
>
> —*Frank Lloyd Wright*

ADMINISTER COMMON SENSE

When Tony got an email from his pastor asking him to serve on the church finance committee, Tony was both honored and baffled.

Honored because in his church of more than 3,000 people, Tony hadn't even realized the pastor knew his name.

And baffled because Tony was a high school senior with precisely zero financial experience. "I have a part-time job, but that's it," says Tony.

Still, if the pastor was asking, Tony was in. "I thought it might be God calling me to a new challenge," he says.

But when Tony showed up for the next committee meeting, he was met with blank stares.

"Turns out the pastor *didn't* know my name. I was the wrong Tony," he laughs. "They apologized, thanked me for caring, and hustled me out the door."

Tony's not angry; he's amused…mostly.

Common sense told Tony he was the wrong guy for the volunteer role he'd been offered. It didn't fit with his experience or natural giftedness. His hunch that there'd been a mix-up was right on target.

God gave Tony what he's given you: common sense. A mind that lets you make a levelheaded assessment about what's what in your life.

The writer of Proverbs had this to say about common sense: "My child, don't lose sight of common sense and discernment. Hang on to them, for they will refresh your soul" (Proverbs 3:21-22).

Consider it a sniff test when you're seeking God's will: Does what you're considering seem like something God would want you to do? As you've gotten to know him, would it make sense for him to be on board with this idea?

Sometimes you may be facing a decision where every option is okay. It's a matter of preference—so make the call. Love God and do what you want.

That said, be aware that sometimes God will ask you to do things that make no sense whatsoever.

Loving your enemies, for instance. In moments when God's clearly expecting you to obey him no matter what you think, follow his lead.

But when he's left it up to you?

Let your common sense be your guide.

PEN-IN-HAND PONDERING

Describe a time trusting your common sense worked out well...and a time it *didn't*.

Common sense is a combination of experience and clear thinking. How would people who know you rank how well your common sense works? Why do you answer as you do?

TALK WITH GOD ABOUT IT

It's tough to grow in your sniff-test abilities regarding God without experiencing him.

Ask Jesus for a creative new way to get to know him better. Then take a 10-minute break from your day to walk through the "Christian Living" section of a local bookstore. As you browse, simply ask Jesus to show you what book to pick—to introduce you to a new way of seeing his heart. And invite Jesus into everyday activities that you normally treat as "no-Jesus" zones—whisper your conversation to him when you're washing dishes or waiting in line or working out at a health club.

Expect him to relate with you, and he will.

DO THIS Whatever came to mind when you asked God about deepening your friendship, *do it*. God's willing to meet you where you are, if you'll issue the invitation.

"
Wait patiently
for the Lord.
Be brave and courageous.
Yes, wait patiently
for the Lord.
"

Psalm 27:14

INSTALL A
DECISION-DELAY BUTTON

When Frank worked as a radio disc jockey, his best friend was the "seven-second button" sitting between two turntables.

"There was a seven-second delay between what happened in the studio and what went on air," Frank explains. "If someone sneezed or swore, I had those few seconds to press the button and save my job."

Because the risk of a stray word causing disaster was so high, Frank kept the button in view at all times. No blocking it with a coffee cup or stack of CDs.

The button failed Frank just once, when another DJ dropped a box of copier paper on his foot.

"Seven seconds wasn't nearly long enough to cover the screaming," says Frank. "I smacked the button twice and then just went to a commercial that played through—twice—before I got the guy out of earshot."

Ever wish life had a seven-second delay button?

You say something and wish you could un-say it. You order that thick slice of pie and immediately regret it—but the waiter has already disappeared.

Just seven seconds. That's all it would take to rethink a decision.

Here's a thought: You can install that button yourself, no wiring required.

And it will help you know—and do—God's will in your life.

Simply get in the habit of pausing before making decisions and inviting the Spirit of Jesus into the process. And this goes not just for the big decisions, but the small ones as well.

Whether to accept that dinner invitation or committee slot. How to respond when you know a difficult conversation has to happen. How to mark a ballot come election time.

Big decisions, small decisions…Jesus is delighted to join you in all of them.

PEN-IN-HAND PONDERING

What's a small decision you made that ended up having big consequences?

_____

_____

_____

_____

_____

_____

_____

_____

How might inviting Jesus into that decision have made a difference?

_____

_____

_____

_____

_____

_____

_____

_____

_____

When Jesus influences a decision you're making, how does he typically do it, and why?

TALK WITH GOD ABOUT IT

Do you really want Jesus involved in your decisions—even the small ones? Perhaps it seems like an imposition on his time (it isn't) or you're making decisions you'd rather he not know about (that's another issue altogether).

Invite Jesus into *all* areas of your life—do it consciously as an experiment for the next 30 days. At the end of that time, note three ways that your life has changed as a result.

DO THIS Using the stopwatch function on your phone or watch, hold your breath for seven seconds. Just seven seconds—the length of a breath or two. The length of a reflection, a glance toward God. A good decision made, or a bad decision avoided.

Just for today, be mindful of giving yourself seven seconds before making a decision. As you pause, invite Jesus to influence your choice. See how it works out.

Then you and Jesus can decide if it's worth doing tomorrow.

BE PATIENT

Janet will be the first to tell you: She's not a patient person.

"I think a six-minute hard-boiled egg takes at least five minutes too long to boil," she says. And that same hurry-up attitude is reflected in her driving.

Or at least it was.

Janet was two cars back at a crosswalk when a pedestrian walking her dog stepped off the curb. "She was taking forever," says Janet, who barely gave the pedestrian a glance. "So I gave the horn a quick honk."

When the woman didn't step up her pace Janet hit the horn again—a longer blast this time.

That's when the woman in the crosswalk turned and Janet could see the white cane. And the vest on the dog.

"I wanted to sink through the pavement," says Janet with a pained expression. "I still do."

Patience may be a virtue, but it's also insanely annoying...especially when you're the one expected to be patient.

You ask Jesus for wisdom in making a decision. You might even ask which option is best. And as the clock ticks down, you find yourself needing to be patient.

So you stop dead in your tracks and wait for a clear signal about what to do.

Which is probably a mistake.

The truth is, God doesn't owe you an answer. Or direction beyond this: If you've prayed about the decision and what appears to be the best course of action is within a biblical and heart-of-Jesus set of boundaries, you're probably good to go.

Make a decision and go with it. It's likely you'll be within God's will.

God's timing isn't necessarily your timing, and that's okay. And if you're making decisions in the context of a friendship with Jesus, he's likely trusting that you'll make an appropriate call, because that call will naturally be influenced by your relationship with him.

PEN-IN-HAND PONDERING

 On a scale of 1 (zero patience) to 10 (patience of a saint), how would you rank yourself? Why? How would others rank you based on how they see you behave behind the wheel or in line? Why?

Describe a time you waited to make a decision because you were waiting for guidance from Jesus. Or describe a time you *wished* you'd waited for guidance from Jesus.

When Jesus doesn't offer his guidance on your timetable, how does that affect your willingness to pray, and why?

TALK WITH GOD ABOUT IT

Be honest: How often do you find yourself growing impatient with God?

You want to follow his lead, but you don't have a crisp, clear understanding of what that is. You ask... ask again...and find yourself waiting.

It's a quick step from patience to impatience to resentment. Where do you land on that continuum?

Talk with Jesus about how you're feeling. It's okay to be honest; you're friends.

DO THIS Practice makes perfect—at least in regards to patience.

For the next several days, practice being patient. Wait for the next elevator. Be generous in letting others merge ahead of you in traffic. Give the latecomers in your life the benefit of the doubt. Notice what you notice about your heart-health when you do this.

And as you're patient with others, take that moment and offer your grateful response to Jesus for being patient with you.

BE WILLING TO ACT

Ron was doing his best to hear and respond to God's voice, to do God's will.

So he was more than a little excited when, driving home from work one day, he felt he heard the voice of God.

"I didn't *think* I heard God speaking to me," says Ron. "I was *sure* of it. And what I heard was this: 'Go three more blocks; then turn left. Go to the yellow house on that street, knock on the door, and tell whoever answers the door about me.'"

Ron's heart nearly pounded through his chest as he counted down the streets.

"I made the turn and then drove slowly down the street. No yellow house on the first block…or the second…or the third. And I'd reached the end of the street."

Ron thought perhaps he'd misunderstood the message. Maybe he was supposed to be looking for yellow trim, so he slowly drove the three blocks again.

Still nothing.

"I thought maybe I'd miscounted streets," says Ron. "I was pretty distracted as I was driving."

The bottom line: Ron drove a grid of five blocks in every direction and couldn't find a yellow house. Not a mustard-colored house, a banana-yellow house, not even a shade of green that might or might not have a hint of yellow in it.

Ron was devastated and at last began to pray. He confessed his frustration at not having clearly heard the message. He poured out his apologies for not being able to do what was asked of him. He felt awful.

"That's when I got a second message," says Ron. "God wasn't actually asking me to find the yellow house; he just wanted to see if I'd be willing to go."

Have people ever asked you for advice and then not taken it?

And then, when the wheels fell off, they were back asking for more advice (which they probably still wouldn't take)?

Welcome to God's world.

Jesus is equally accustomed to people not doing what he tells them to do. Give away your riches and follow me, he says to a wealthy man who then walks away. Trust me, he tells crowds who yawn and drift off after the miracles stop. Have faith, he says to people whose faith never stretches to include him.

Time after time Jesus is ignored, just as his Father is ignored.

Here are three reasons you might not want to join that parade.

First, when you ask Jesus to make his will clear to you and he does just that, you have no excuses. You asked, and he answered. It's now a matter of obedience.

Plus, you're straining your relationship with Jesus. How many times can your friends ignore you before you get the message: They're not all that into you? Is that a message you really want to be sending to Jesus?

And, finally, there's this: Calling yourself a follower of Jesus requires that you actually...you know...*follow Jesus.* As in, act on what you discover he wants you to do.

James wrote this: "But don't just listen to God's word. You must do what it says. Otherwise, you are only fooling yourselves" (James 1:22).

When you're seeking God's will, there's no room for self-deception, only time for truth—for speaking truth, hearing truth, and acting on truth.

PEN-IN-HAND PONDERING

Describe a time you had a strong feeling about something (perhaps an injustice or a political candidate) and you didn't act on it. Why did you stay on the sidelines?

_____

_____

_____

_____

_____

_____

_____

Write about a time you *did* act. What was the situation—and how did it work out?

_____

_____

_____

_____

_____

_____

_____

_____

_____

_____

_____

_____

Describe a time you acted on what you thought was God's prompting. Looking back, do you think you were right to act...or not? Why?

TALK WITH GOD ABOUT IT

Acting on what you discover about God's will is often hard because it requires that you change somehow. Change a habit, an addiction, or an attitude.

And change is hard.

Do this: Have a conversation with Jesus about you and his will. If you're out of alignment, ask what might need to change. Ask for the courage to confront that change and for his help getting through it.

DO THIS Adopt an "I'm in" attitude for the next few days. Where you see a problem, do what you can to solve it. When you see someone who could use a hug, be willing to step outside your comfort zone and offer one (but not in a creepy way). If you see a situation that could benefit from prayer, pause and pray.

Then consider this: How is switching your default setting to being willing to act on nudges from God changing your life?

"

Don't let your
hearts be troubled.
Trust in God,
and trust also
in me.

"

—JESUS
John 14:1

POSTSCRIPT

Remember that knock, knock, knock Jesus-story we referenced earlier? It's one of his parables that doesn't show up often in sermons because...well, see for yourself...

"Suppose you went to a friend's house at midnight, wanting to borrow three loaves of bread. You say to him, 'A friend of mine has just arrived for a visit, and I have nothing for him to eat.'

"And suppose he calls out from his bedroom, 'Don't bother me. The door is locked for the night, and my family and I are all in bed. I can't help you.'

"But I tell you this—though he won't do it for friendship's sake, if you keep knocking long enough, he will get up and give you whatever you need because of your shameless persistence.

"And so I tell you, keep on asking, and you will receive what you ask for. Keep on seeking, and you will find. Keep on knocking, and the door will be opened to you.

"For everyone who asks, receives. Everyone who seeks, finds. And to everyone who knocks, the door will be opened" (Luke 11:5-10).

Jesus is teaching about prayer…and persistence.

And the story appears to paint God as a grumpy guy who'd rather pelt you with rocks from his bedroom window than trudge downstairs to fetch you a few loaves of bread.

Not a comfortable image.

And yet, it's perfect. It's the perfect parable.

Why? Because Jesus is saying it's okay to ask and keep asking. To expect that, sooner or later, the bread will be delivered to the door.

So keep knocking as you seek to grow in your relationship with God, a friendship in which you come to know God more intimately.

Keep seeking God's will for your life.

And keep asking. Your questions aren't going unnoticed, even at midnight.